EDGE
BOOKS

BUG WARS

SCORPION vs. CENTIPEDE

BY KIMBERLY FELTES TAYLOR

DUEL TO THE DEATH

CONSULTANT:
Christiane Weirauch
Professor of Entomology,
Department of Entomology
University of California, Riverside

CAPSTONE PRESS
a capstone imprint

Edge Books are published by Capstone Press,
1710 Roe Crest Drive, North Mankato, Minnesota 56003
www.mycapstone.com

Library of Congress Cataloging-in-Publication Data
Feltes Taylor, Kimberly, author.
  Scorpion vs. centipede : duel to the death / by Kimberly Feltes Taylor.
    pages cm. -- (Edge. Bug wars)
Audience: Ages 9-10.
Audience: Grades 4 to 6.
Summary: "Describes the characteristics of bark scorpions and giant centipedes, and
what may happen when these bugs encounter one another in nature"-- Provided by
publisher.
ISBN 978-1-4914-8066-3 (library binding)
ISBN 978-1-4914-8070-0 (pbk.)
1. Centruroides--Juvenile literature. 2. Scorpions--Juvenile literature. 3. Centipedes--
Juvenile literature. I. Title. II. Title: Scorpion versus centipede.
QL458.72.B8F45 2016
  595--dc23
                                        2015024332

Editorial Credits
Nate LeBoutillier, editor; Russell Griesmer, designer; Katy LaVigne, production specialist

Photo Credits
Alamy: PhotoStock-Israel, 25; Corbis: RooM the Agency/DeepDesertPhoto (RF), 23; Corel,
19 (bottom); Dreamstime: Daniel Mccauley Iv, 29; Getty Images: Digital Vision, 7 (bottom),
15 (bottom), 17 (bottom); Nature Picture Library: Barry Mansell, 27; Science Source:
Tom McHugh, 19 (top); Shutterstock: Aleksey Stemmer, Cover, 4, 11 (top), 21, Audrey
Snider-Bell, 9 (top), 13 (left), c photospirit, 7, (top), IrinaK, 15 (top), Kittikorn Phongok, 13
(right), RPan Xunbin, 17 (top); Visuals Unlimited/Gerold & Cynthia Merker, Cover, 5, 11
(bottom), 20; Wikimedia: Canley, 9 (bottom)

Design Elements
Capstone and Shutterstock:

Printed and bound in US.
007521CGS16

TABLE OF CONTENTS

WELCOME TO BUG WARS!

Bugs can be ferocious! Some of them have claws and stingers. Others have mouths as sharp as razors. Some even have fangs. They use these weapons to hunt down—and kill—other bugs. Sometimes, they easily crush their **prey**. Other times, they must fight head to head. The fight can end with either bug as the winner.

prey—an animal hunted by another animal for food

nocturnal—active at night and resting during the day

arthropod—an animal with a hard outer shell and many legs with joints

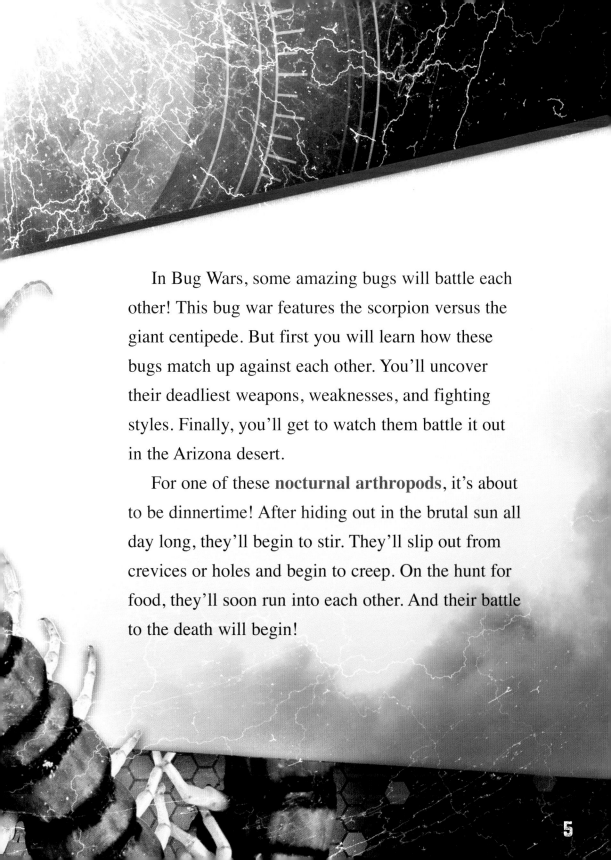

In Bug Wars, some amazing bugs will battle each other! This bug war features the scorpion versus the giant centipede. But first you will learn how these bugs match up against each other. You'll uncover their deadliest weapons, weaknesses, and fighting styles. Finally, you'll get to watch them battle it out in the Arizona desert.

For one of these **nocturnal arthropods**, it's about to be dinnertime! After hiding out in the brutal sun all day long, they'll begin to stir. They'll slip out from crevices or holes and begin to creep. On the hunt for food, they'll soon run into each other. And their battle to the death will begin!

THE COMBATANTS

The bark scorpion and the giant centipede are both found in northern Mexico and the southwestern part of the United States. But they are most commonly spotted in the Arizona desert. These two creatures prey on a wide variety of bugs, including each other. When they meet up, they almost always fight—often to the death!

The battle between these two well-matched arthropods can be lengthy. One reason for the long death matches is that both bugs have **exoskeletons**, or outside skeletons. Humans have endoskeletons, or skeletons inside their bodies. These bugs' hard outer skeletons help protect them like armor during battle.

FIERCE FACT

THERE ARE MORE THAN 1,500 SPECIES OF SCORPION AND MORE THAN 3,000 SPECIES OF CENTIPEDES.

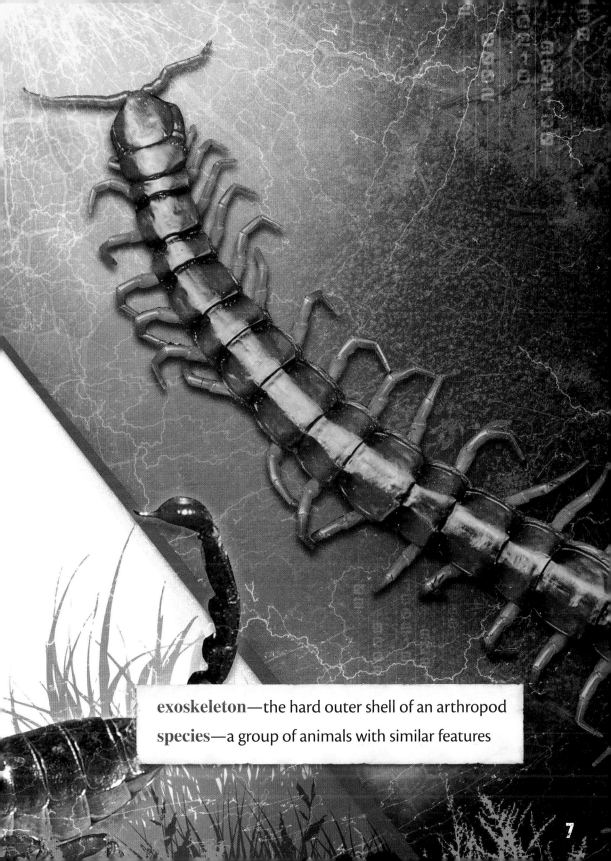

exoskeleton—the hard outer shell of an arthropod

species—a group of animals with similar features

SIZE

The bark scorpion grows up to 3 inches (7.6 centimeters) long. That might sound tiny. But the bark scorpion would probably stretch across the full width of your palm. (Now imagine this deadly creature scurrying up your arm and ready to sting. It doesn't sound so tiny now, does it?) Compared to other bugs, the bark scorpion is big. Most species of termites, beetles, spiders, and many other bugs do not even grow to be 1 inch (2.5 cm) long.

The giant centipede is called a "giant" for good reason. It grows up to 8 inches (20 cm) long. That's huge in the world of bugs! With extra length comes extra weight. So the giant centipede has more power than smaller bugs. In a giant centipede's battle with a bark scorpion, the centipede has the size advantage.

But don't count the scorpion out. All that extra centipede length just means one thing to the fearless scorpion—more to grab onto with its pincers!

RATING

1.5

SCORPION:
tiny trooper

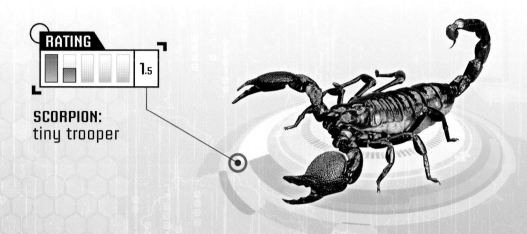

RATING

3.5

CENTIPEDE:
super squiggly

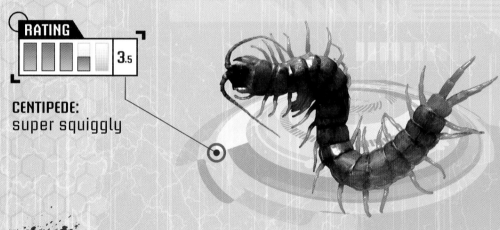

FIERCE FACT

THE LARGEST SCORPION IS THE EMPEROR SCORPION.
IT GROWS UP TO 8 INCHES (20 CM) LONG. IT LIVES IN
WESTERN AFRICA. THE AMAZONIAN CENTIPEDE, THE
LARGEST CENTIPEDE, GROWS UP TO 14 INCHES (35 CM)
IN LENGTH AND IS FOUND IN SOUTH AMERICA.

9

SPEED AND AGILITY

The bark scorpion is speedy when it wants to be. Its legs are jointed. So it can quickly move forward—or even leap—to attack.

The bark scorpion's legs end in claws. These claws help it move nimbly over sand, rocks, or objects in its path. No terrain is too tough for this deadly creature.

The giant centipede is also a fast mover. Most have 21 to 23 pairs of legs, giving them **agility**. Each pair of legs works together, and the pairs move in waves. In this way, centipedes can appear to slither like a snake.

Unlike the scorpion, the centipede cannot move its entire body to the right or the left in just one or two steps. But it does move sideways more often than the scorpion. To go sideways, the centipede curves its head left or right to set a new direction. Then the body follows.

agility—the ability to move quickly and easily

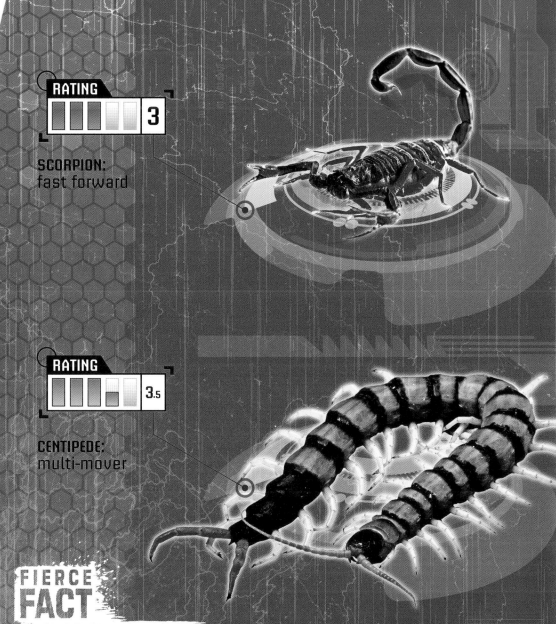

RATING

					3

SCORPION:
fast forward

RATING

					3.5

CENTIPEDE:
multi-mover

FIERCE FACT

HOUSE CENTIPEDES ARE VERY FAST BUT GROW TO JUST
1.5 INCHES (3.8 CM) LONG. THEY LIVE IN BASEMENTS,
BATHROOMS, AND CLOSETS. THEY EAT OTHER INSECTS,
SUCH AS BED BUGS AND TERMITES, THAT YOU REALLY
DON'T WANT LIVING IN YOUR HOUSE.

WEAPONS

The bark scorpion's first deadly weapons are **pincers**. The pincers are located on either side of its head. The scorpion uses its pincers to grab and crush smaller prey. With larger prey, the scorpion uses its pincers to hold. This keeps prey from running away or fighting back.

The scorpion has a second deadly weapon—a stinger. The stinger is located at the end of the scorpion's tail. It plunges the stinger into prey and releases venom, **paralyzing** the prey. Then the scorpion starts to eat the prey alive.

The giant centipede uses its fangs for a weapon. The fangs look like its first pair of legs. But they are not legs. After the centipede bites into prey, it releases venom through its fangs. The venom numbs the prey and poisons the prey's **nervous system**. The prey stops moving and dies.

The giant centipede's many legs are another weapon. It uses its legs to grab and hold, like the scorpion uses its **pincers**.

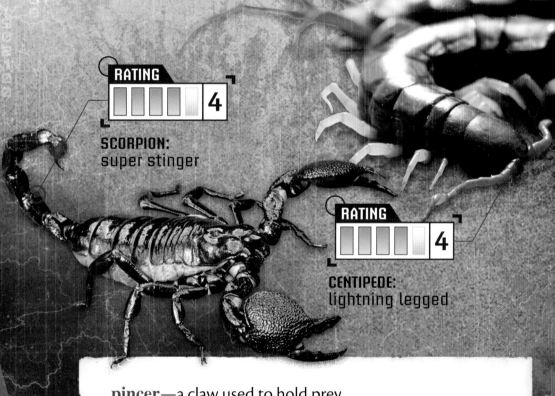

SCORPION VENOM CAN BE DEADLY TO HUMANS—BUT IT IS ALSO PROVING TO BE HELPFUL. THE VENOM FROM SOME SCORPIONS CAN BE USED AS "TUMOR PAINT." THE VENOM IS USED TO LOCATE CANCER CELLS IN A HUMAN. THEN A SURGEON OPERATES AND REMOVES THE CANCER CELLS.

RATING 4

SCORPION:
super stinger

RATING 4

CENTIPEDE:
lightning legged

pincer—a claw used to hold prey

paralyze—to cause a loss of ability to control the muscles

nervous system—the brain, the spinal cord, and nerves; the nervous system controls all body functions

DEFENSES

The bark scorpion's main defense is its yellow-brown color. This creature is not easy to see when on rock, sand, dirt, and—of course—tree bark.

What happens if a **predator** spots the bark scorpion? The scorpion adopts a threatening pose. It spreads its pincers wide. It raises its stinger high into the air. It hopes to scare off the predator.

The giant centipede uses color as a defense too. But not to hide. Rather, its red and black body and yellow legs are meant to look threatening.

Furthermore, the coloring makes the head and tail look alike. So predators don't know which end to attack. If they attack the tail, the centipede can quickly curl its head around and dig its fangs into the predator.

The giant centipede can also easily curl up to avoid attack. The centipede is very **flexible** because of its many segments. This flexibility gives the giant centipede the advantage in defenses.

predator—an animal that hunts other animals for food
flexible—able to bend

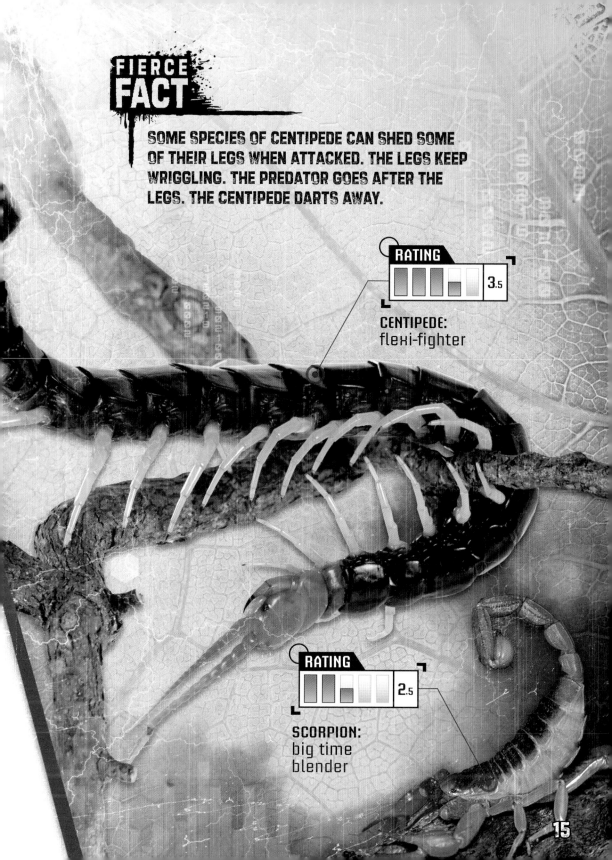

SOME SPECIES OF CENTIPEDE CAN SHED SOME OF THEIR LEGS WHEN ATTACKED. THE LEGS KEEP WRIGGLING. THE PREDATOR GOES AFTER THE LEGS. THE CENTIPEDE DARTS AWAY.

RATING 3.5

CENTIPEDE:
flexi-fighter

RATING 2.5

SCORPION:
big time
blender

WEAKNESSES

The bark scorpion can have up to six pairs of eyes. But it has poor vision. It can only tell if it is dark or light out.

To "see," the bark scorpion relies on its sense of touch. Scorpions have sensors called **sensilla**. The sensilla is located mostly on the legs and body. The sensilla help scorpions feel the shaking of the ground when something moves. This shaking lets the scorpion know where things are and if they are coming or going.

The giant centipede also has poor vision. Like the bark scorpion, its eyes can only tell light from dark. So it relies mostly on its antennae to feel and smell prey and predators. The **antennae** are long, agile, and in constant motion.

Unlike the bark scorpion, the giant centipede does not have any sensors. It only has its antennae. So the giant centipede is the slight loser when it comes to weaknesses.

antennae—feelers on the head of an insect or arthropod used to sense movement

sensilla—a simple sense organ consisting of one or a few cells at the end of a sensory nerve fiber

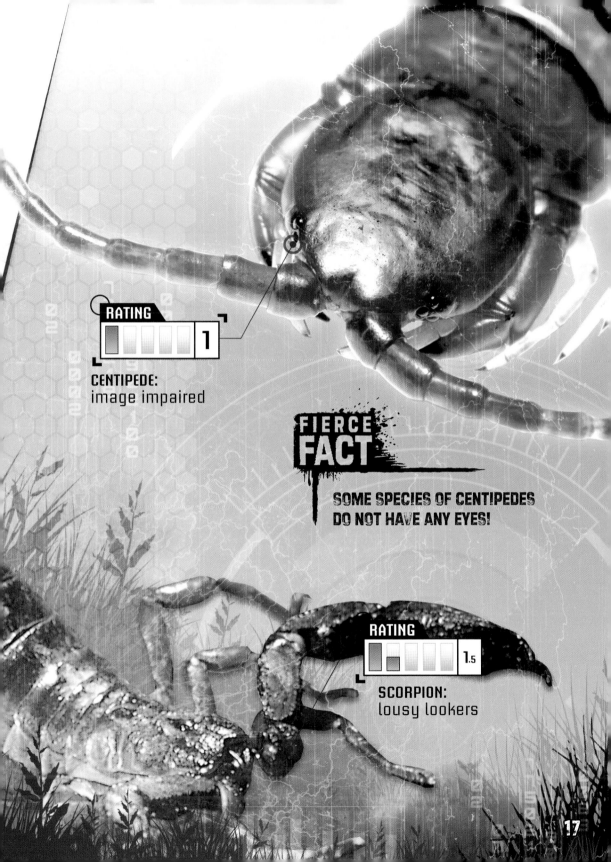

RATING 1

CENTIPEDE:
image impaired

FIERCE FACT

SOME SPECIES OF CENTIPEDES
DO NOT HAVE ANY EYES!

RATING 1.5

SCORPION:
lousy lookers

ATTACK STYLE

The bark scorpion hunts alone. First, it finds a place to sit and wait for prey. If prey moves toward the scorpion, it stays very still. The scorpion wants prey to come as close as possible. When the prey is close enough, the scorpion lunges. It grabs onto the prey with its pincers. If needed, it uses its stinger. Then the scorpion starts to eat.

The giant centipede is also a lone hunter. But unlike the scorpion, it doesn't wait around for prey. It seeks it out. Once it detects prey, the centipede moves quickly toward it. The centipede grabs onto the prey with its fangs. It releases its venom. It might curl its body around the prey to keep it still until the venom kicks in. Even so, the scorpion's surprise-attack method gives it the slight advantage.

FIERCE FACT

SCORPIONS ARE CANNIBALS. THEY WILL EAT OTHER SCORPIONS—EVEN THEIR OWN FAMILY MEMBERS!

RATING

3.5

CENTIPEDE:
heroic hunter

RATING

3

SCORPION:
surprise stalker

19

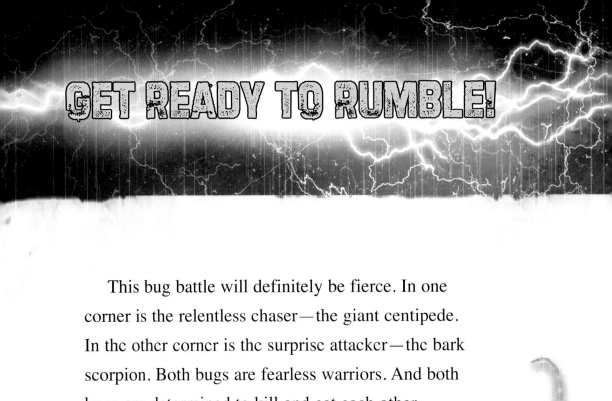

GET READY TO RUMBLE!

This bug battle will definitely be fierce. In one corner is the relentless chaser—the giant centipede. In thc othcr corncr is thc surprisc attackcr—thc bark scorpion. Both bugs are fearless warriors. And both bugs are determined to kill and eat each other.

BEFORE THE BATTLE BEGINS . . .

This battle is made-up, just like your favorite movie. But the battle could happen in real life. These two types of bugs really do hunt each other. They really do fight. And each time, one of the bugs really does win.

Now, for our battle. Who will win? And who will end up as dinner?

HUNT TO THE DEATH!

The sun has almost set in the Arizona desert. Ironwood trees and cacti cast long shadows in the last of the dim light. The bark scorpion—ready to eat—crawls out of a crevice in a rock wall. It scurries down the wall. It starts to wander along a dusty path. The path is lined with pebbles and short shrub. It has no trouble hopping around, or even over, these obstacles.

Suddenly, the scorpion stops. Its sensors have picked up movement. It backs up and hides just behind a rock. There it waits.

Just a few rocks to the right, a giant centipede is slowly wriggling along another path. It has no idea that it is headed toward the scorpion.

FIERCE FACT

PREGNANT FEMALE SCORPIONS ARE THE FIERCEST. THE EXTRA WEIGHT THEY CARRY WITH THE PREGNANCY MAKES IT DIFFICULT FOR THEM TO SCURRY AWAY FROM PREDATORS. SO THEY ARE QUICK TO USE THEIR STINGERS.

FIRST STRIKE

The scorpion waits, keeping very still. The centipede comes into the scorpion's sight. The centipede keeps moving along its path, still unaware of the scorpion. At just the right moment, the scorpion lunges but misses.

The centipede, using its antenna to quickly locate the scorpion, veers toward the scorpion, ready for a fight. The scorpion takes an offensive pose—pincers spread, stinger raised. But the centipede doesn't pause. It zooms toward the scorpion.

The scorpion hops left and right to dodge the centipede. Recognizing the perfect moment, the scorpion springs toward the centipede again—this time, with success! It grabs onto the centipede's head with its pincers. The centipede can't possibly dig its fangs into the scorpion under this grip.

But the centipede isn't ready to give up. It coils around the scorpion defensively, ready to squeeze the scorpion with its entire body. Can the scorpion out-wrestle the centipede?

THE GIANT AMAZONIAN CENTIPEDE IS SO FIERCE AND POWERFUL THAT IT CAN CATCH BATS IN MID-FLIGHT.

CHARGE!

The scorpion knows it is in a bad position. It flings the centipede away before the centipede can wrap its body around him. The centipede crashes against a rock and is briefly stunned. The scorpion takes advantage of this moment and charges at the centipede's head again.

But the scorpion has mistaken the centipede's tail for its head. The scorpion lunges at the wrong end. This mistake gives the centipede time to recover. It quickly curls its head toward the scorpion, ready to dig its fangs into the scorpion.

The scorpion senses the error, though. It quickly changes plans and scurries up the rock wall. Then, it circles back around and hovers over the centipede. The scorpion lunges again—this time, at the centipede's mid-section. It catches the centipede and digs in with its pincers.

The centipede once again curls its head around toward the scorpion. The centipede wants to dig its fangs into the scorpion and release its venom.

MOST SPECIES OF CENTIPEDES ARE HARMLESS TO HUMANS. BUT THE GIANT CENTIPEDE WILL BITE HUMANS. THE BITE CAN BE PAINFUL, THOUGH NOT DEADLY.

A FINAL STING

The centipede's fangs come closer and closer
to the scorpion. But the scorpion does not let go.
Instead, once again, it waits. When the centipede's
head—and fangs—are very close, the scorpion
whips its tail around. It plunges its stinger into the
centipede's head. The scorpion's venom quickly takes
effect. The centipede is paralyzed and lies motionless.
It's a victory for the scorpion!

Now that the scorpion has captured its dinner,
it must prepare the meal. It tears the centipede into
pieces. It spits digestive juices on each piece. The
digestive juices break down the centipede pieces
into mush. After the digestive juices have done their
job, the scorpion begins to suck up the mush. A slow
eater, the scorpion enjoys its meal for hours.

FIERCE FACT

IN GREEK MYTHOLOGY, A GIANT SCORPION NAMED SCORPIO KILLED THE GREAT HUNTER ORION. WHEN THE GODS PUT THEM IN THE SKY AS CONSTELLATIONS, OR GROUPS OF STARS, THEY PUT THEM FAR APART. THIS KEPT SCORPIO AND ORION FROM FIGHTING.

GLOSSARY

agility (uh-JILL-uh-tee)—the ability to move quickly in a variety of ways

antennae (an-THE-nay)—a pair of long, thin feelers on an insect's headt

detect (di-TEKT)—to sense or discover something
exoskeleton (ek-soh-SKE-luh-tuhn)—a structure on the outside of an animal that gives it support

flexible (FLEK-suh-buhl)—able to bend without breaking

nervous system (NUR-vuhss SISS-tuhm)—the brain, the spinal cord, and the ability for the brain to communicate with the body

nocturnal (nahk-TUR-nuhl)—active at night

paralyze (PAY-ruh-lize)—to cause to become unable to move

pincer (PIN-sur)—a claw-like body part

predator (PRED-uh-tur)—an animal that hunts other animals for food

prey (PRAY)—an animal hunted by another animal for food

sensilla (sen-SILL-ah)—a simple sense organ consisting of one or a few cells at the end of a sensory nerve fiber

species (SPEE-sheez)—a scientific grouping of plants or animals that have many common characteristics

READ MORE

Elkin, Matthew. *20 Fun Facts About Centipedes.* New York: Gareth Stevens Publishing, 2011.

Markle, Sandra. *Scorpions: Armored Stingers.* Minneapolis, Minn.: Lerner Publications Company, 2011.

Pringle, Laurence. *Scorpions! Strange and Wonderful.* Honesdale, Penn.: Boyds Mills Press, Inc., 2013.

INTERNET SITES

FactHound offers a safe, fun way to find Internet sites related to this book. All of the sites on FactHound have been researched by our staff.

Here's all you do:

Visit *www.facthound.com*

Type in this code: 9781491480663

Check out projects, games and lots more at
www.capstonekids.com

INDEX